BEYONDBURNOUT

45 Day Journal

Cynthia Howard RN, CNC, PhD

"Start with one small change in your day.
Before you know it, you will feel more energized and ready for anything ..."

—Dr. Cynthia Howard

CONTENTS

Day 1: Set a Goal

As a result of this 45-day plan I want to:

_____

_____

_____

_____

Describe your day as a result of achieving your goal:

_____

_____

_____

_____

_____

_____

As a result of my new day, I will feel:

_____

_____

_____

_____

_____

Daily Review:

What worked?

_____

_____

_____

_____

What did not?

_____

_____

_____

_____

What's Next?

_____

_____

_____

_____

Day 2: Breathe

Breathe deliberately. Practice "Going to Neutral," 1 minute – 5 times a day. The following are times you can practice this.

1. Brushing my teeth.
2. Walking into work.
3. Right before eating my lunch.
4. As I am leaving work.
5. Right before bed.

How did this impact my day?

_____

_____

_____

Optional: Color while practicing "Getting to Neutral."

Daily Review:

What worked?

_____

_____

_____

_____

What did not?

_____

_____

_____

_____

What's Next?

_____

_____

_____

_____

Day 3: Drink more water

Water is a natural energizer. It flushes out toxins and plumps up mucus membranes. When tired, drink 4 ounces of water.

Here are the 5 best times to drink water.

1. Drink 32 ounces before your first cup of coffee.

2. Drink 8 ounces 30 minutes before a meal.

3. When you are hungry.

4. Before and during your workout.

5. Before you go to sleep.

Your body loses water while you sleep and having some water before you go to bed has been noted to reduce risk of heart issues.

Variety:

Infuse water with fresh mint, strawberries, cucumber, lemon, essential oil of peppermint, citrus ... endless possibilities!

What did you notice by increasing your water?

Daily Review:

What worked?

What did not?

What's Next?

Day 4: Practice

Practice "Getting to Neutral," and increase water by 8 ounces.

Examples:

1. Drink 4 ounces before you get ready for work.

2. Drink 4 ounces before lunch.

3. Drink 2 ounces before your meetings.

4. Before and during your workout.

5. Before you go to sleep.

Mind Map your plan:

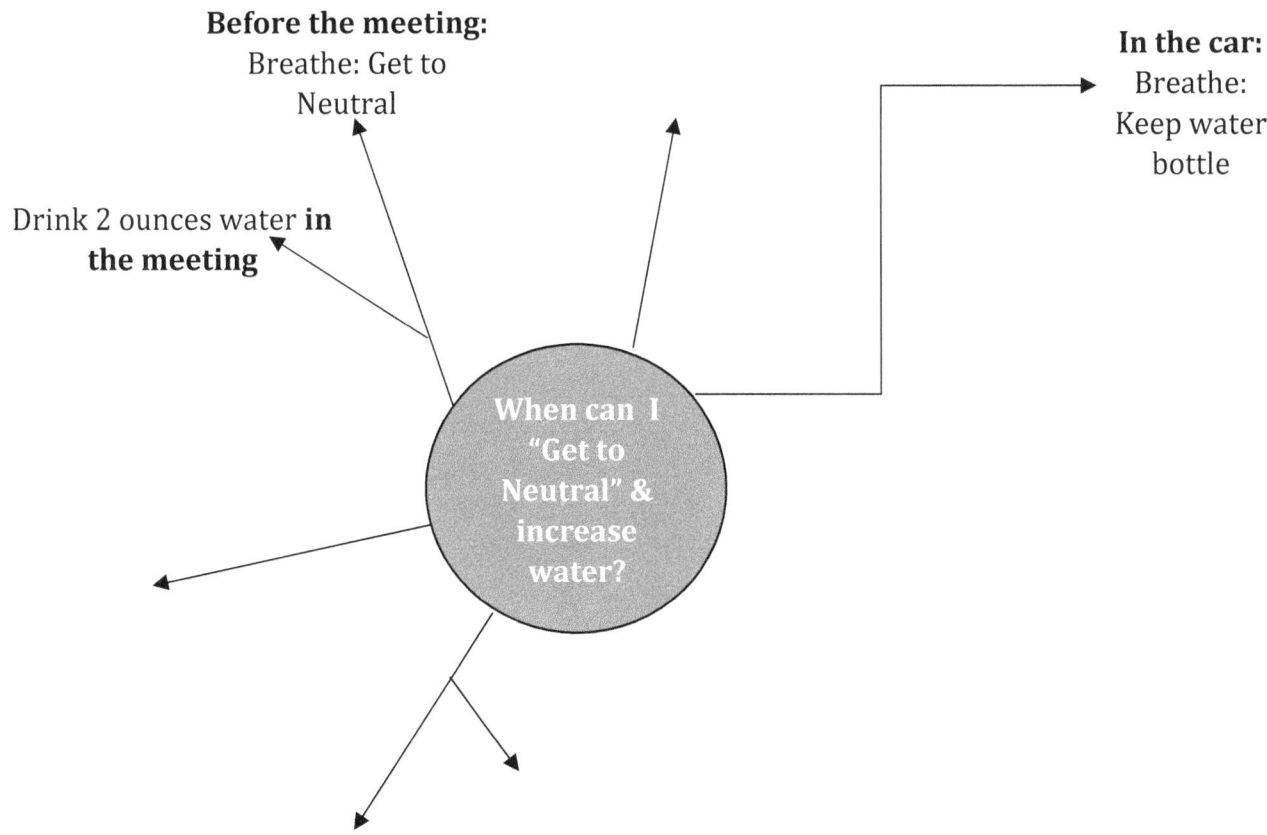

Daily Review:

What worked?

What did not?

What's next?

Day 5: Practice

Continue to use these simple suggestions and integrate them into your day. As you do, you are increasing your mindfulness.

What have you noticed?

_____

_____

_____

_____

_____

Color or Doodle:

Weekly Review:

What worked?

What did not?

What's next?

Day 6 & 7: A Mindful Weekend

This is your time to connect with family friends and yourself! Schedule in your chores (4 hours) and then leave the rest of the time to nurture yourself and your life.

Weekends need to have a slower pace than weekdays. This is how you recharge. I recommend practicing mindfulness on the weekend to rejuvenate you, and also prepare you to be more mindful at work when the pace is faster and more complex.

Nurturing Activities and Opportunities to Practice Mindfulness:

1. Time outside in parks, near a lake or at the beach.
2. Church and faith related activities to worship.
3. Lunch with a friend.
4. Brunch with your family.
5. Cooking: washing, chopping, cooking fresh vegetables, stews, soups, salads.
6. Driving through the countryside; short day trips.
7. 15 minutes of stretching and deep breathing.
8. Power walk, 30 minutes, breaking a sweat.
9. A round of golf, non-competitive.
10. Playing board games with family and friends.
11. Reading without interruption for at least 20 minutes.
12. Using essential oils with any deep breathing activities.
13. Heart Lock-in®5-15 minutes in the morning. Send yourself loving energy first and then extend it outward.
14. Make love.
15. Spend quality time with your children.
16. Walk your dog. Throw a ball. Give him a treat. Enjoy their unconditional love.
17. Dress up. Put on your best, do your hair, make-up. Pretend it is a first date. Surprise someone you love.
18. Buy flowers. Spend 10 minutes arranging them in a vase and display them in your home. Admire them and feel the gratitude for their beauty and presence.
19. Take a bath with mineral salts and essential oil of lavender. Breathe slowly and deeply, release the tension.
20. Wander through antique shops, looking at the objects, repurpose them. How might they be used in a new and different way?

Notice, none of these activities include a screen or a plug.

Day 8: Manage Interruptions

We live in the age of distraction. This new normal has been shown to be physically and mentally draining. Keep this interruption log for the day to identify your interruptions.

Date/ Time	Interruption	Time of interr- uption	Time to get back to task	Did you lose your focus?
3/21 2pm	*EXAMPLES: Email from Boss*	*13 min.*	*6 min.*	*Yes*
4pm	*Checked my Twitter account*	*20 min*	*Did not get back to it.*	*Yes*

Date/ Time	Interruption	Time of interruption	Time to get back to task	Did you lose your focus?

Daily Review:

What worked?

_____

_____

_____

_____

What did not?

_____

_____

_____

_____

What's next?

_____

_____

_____

_____

Day 9: 20 Minutes Uninterrupted Time

Today plan to have 20 minutes of time when you can read, without interruption. Turn off your phone and all your distractions for a minimum of 20 minutes. Research has found this activity to improve concentration. Close your door so you will not be disturbed.

Jot down any thoughts or experiences that resist this idea:

Daily Review:

What worked?

_____

_____

_____

_____

What did not?

_____

_____

_____

_____

What's next?

_____

_____

_____

_____

Day 10: Practice

Continue to schedule in 20 minutes of uninterrupted time. Practice "Getting to Neutral," read, sip water. You can also choose to color during this time. No devices. Unplug.

What have you noticed?

_____

_____

_____

_____

Color or Doodle:

Daily Review:

What worked?

What did not?

What's next?

Day 11: Practice

Continue to schedule in 20 minutes of uninterrupted time. Practice "Getting to Neutral," read, sip water. You can also choose to color during this time. No devices. Unplug.

What have you noticed?

_____

_____

_____

_____

_____

Color or Doodle:

Daily Review:

What worked?

What did not?

What's next?

Day 12: Practice

Continue to schedule in 20 minutes of uninterrupted time. Practice "Getting to Neutral," read, sip water. You can also choose to color during this time. No devices. Unplug.

What have you noticed?

_____

_____

_____

_____

Color or Doodle:

Weekly Review:

What worked?

What did not?

What's next?

Day 13 & 14: Energizing Weekend

This is your time to regroup and recharge. Weekends are your time. Do you need to reclaim this time from chores, family demands or your own "to-do" list?

Keep in mind, weekends need to have a slower pace than weekdays. This is how you rejuvenate. Write down all those activities that energize you. Highlight those you commit to doing this weekend.

Day 15: Attitude of Gratitude

Gratitude is one of those emotions that triggers a flood of helpful hormones throughout the body. When you regularly engage in gratitude thinking, you will flip a switch in the brain, increasing your perspective. There is more to gratitude than simply feeling good.

Too often, everyday life with its compulsive busyness makes it difficult to feel grateful. Use the timer on your phone and do a brain dump. Write down everything you are grateful for, large and small; do not over think this. You want to have a reference list for those times you may be stressed or frustrated and blocked to what may be going well in your life.

Write out everything you feel grateful for in the next 3 minutes:

Daily Review:

What worked?

What did not?

What's next?

Day 16: Heart Lock-in®

Today transition from the breathing technique, "Getting to Neutral," to the Heart Lock-in. This practice is quite powerful. The results are subtle; however, they will be profound with continued practice. Start with one-minute increments and work up to 5 minutes in the morning; 15 minutes cumulative throughout the day.

Instructions

Step 1:

Focus your attention in the area of the heart. Imagine your breath is flowing in and out of your heart or chest area, breathing a little slower and deeper than usual.

Step 2:

Activate and sustain a regenerative feeling such as appreciation, care or compassion.

Step 3:

Radiate that renewing feeling to yourself and others.

Sustain that feeling for as long as you can working in 1-minute increments.

When will you use this technique during your day? Write out those times:

_____

_____

_____

_____

_____

Daily Review:

What worked?

What did not?

What's next?

Day 17: Practice

Continue to use the Heart Lock in. Keep track of the time you are able to practice.

Write out a short description of how you felt after using this technique:

_____

_____

_____

_____

_____

_____

Daily Review:

What worked?

_____

_____

_____

_____

What did not?

_____

_____

_____

_____

What's next?

_____

_____

_____

_____

Day 18: Practice

Continue to use the Heart Lock in. Keep track of the time you are able to practice.

Write out a short description of how you felt after using this technique:

Daily Review:

What worked?

_____

_____

_____

_____

What did not?

_____

_____

_____

_____

What's next?

_____

_____

_____

_____

Day 19: Practice

Continue to use the Heart Lock in. Keep track of the time you are able to practice.

Write out a short description of how you felt after using this technique:

_____

_____

_____

_____

_____

_____

Weekly Review:

What worked?

What did not?

What's next?

Day 20 & 21 An Adventurous Weekend

Weekends are designed to be your time to recharge. If you are in a rut and tend to do the same thing every weekend, it may be time to change it up. Here are some suggestions to mix up your weekend.

1. Day trip to local town. Enjoy the drive. Stop to walk, hike, see historic sights. Pack a healthy picnic lunch.
2. Look for cheap flights and fly out Friday night to a fun city. Come back Sunday night. Take a carry on, only. Travel light.
3. Play a "murder mystery" with your family. Give them clues and spend the early evening, acting in the mystery. Enjoy finger food after the event and talk about it.
4. Look for a local "Escape" room in your area and take friends or family.
5.
6.
7.
8.
9.
10.

Write in ideas you have thought about, but, have yet to act upon. Now is your time. Weekends need to restore you. Getting quality sleep and eating healthy food is important, and you also need enjoyable stimulation. Sleeping the weekend away is not going to restore you, over the long term.

Stay balanced!

Day 23: Confront Your Elephants

Elephants are those issues that get bigger and heavier when you ignore them.

Make a list of the issues, personal and work related, that you have ignored:

Daily Review:

What worked?

What did not?

What's next?

Day 24: Pick an Elephant

Review your list and pick one of the elephants you want to confront. Write out how it has impacted you and how life can change if you deal with it. Spell out a simple plan to face it.

How has this elephant impacted your life?

_____

_____

_____

_____

How will life be different without it?

_____

_____

_____

_____

What is your plan to eat this elephant?

_____

_____

_____

_____

Facing your elephants can feel scary and big – that is why it is an elephant! I can promise you by facing one at a time, and using an incremental process, you will defeat it. Let's look at an example.

Common elephants include overindulging in food, alcohol, spending money etc. Let's say Mari wants to cut down on overeating desserts. She has gained over 20 pounds and hates how she looks in her clothes. This has kept her from stepping out in meetings and sharing her ideas.

Breaking down your elephant:

The "elephant" of overeating is a big issue. Instead identify an issue within overeating you can tackle in the next 3 days – overeating sweets. Mari has a cola drink in the morning, and cookies at lunch, and pie with her family at night.

How the elephant has impacted her life:

Mari struggles with her weight and as a result struggles with confidence. Every time she gives in to her cravings, she has more self-doubt. By confronting her elephants, she can stop this roller coaster that is blocking forward momentum in her career.

Without the sweets, Mari knows she will avoid the energy slump she has every afternoon, and she will lose weight. She will also increase her confidence in her ability to follow through on her goals.

How her life will be different:

Without the distraction of snacking, she will have more energy and less brain fog. Mari can see herself slimmer and less preoccupied with food.

Her plan to eat the elephant:

Mari is going to switch to water in the morning. She will be naturally energized and without this sugar surge in the morning, she may crave less in the afternoon. She decided to walk for 10 minutes at lunch with a friend. This will satisfy her "mouth hunger" for something fun and need for socialization. She will enjoy pie (for now) with her family at night.

She will evaluate how it went after 3 days and then come up with a new plan.

Daily Review:

What worked?

What did not?

What's next?

Day 25: Eat the Elephant

Continue to use the plan you prescribed to confront your elephant. Stay consistent. Write out those thoughts and resistant thoughts that block you from following through.

Write out your self-talk as it relates to your plan to confront your elephant:

_____

_____

_____

_____

_____

_____

Mind map the impact of your elephant:

> Your
> Elephant

Daily Review:

What worked?

What did not?

What's next?

Day 26: Eat the Elephant

Continue to use the plan you prescribed to confront your elephant. Stay consistent. Write out those thoughts and urges to resist or stop your follow through.

Write out your self-talk as it relates to your plan to confront your elephant:

_____

_____

_____

_____

_____

_____

Mind map the impact of your elephant:

Your
Elephant

Daily Review:

What worked?

What did not?

What's next?

Day 27: Eat the Elephant

Continue to use the plan you prescribed to confront your elephant. Stay consistent. Write out those thoughts and urges to resist or stop your follow through.

Write out your self-talk as it relates to your plan to confront your elephant:

_____

_____

_____

_____

_____

_____

Mind map the impact of your elephant:

Your
Elephant

Weekly Review:

What worked?

What did not?

What's next?

Day 28 & 29: Design Your Weekend

Write your plan for your ideal weekend. Script it exactly as you want to spend the weekend. Do not think about what others may want. Describe YOUR ideal weekend.

_____

_____

_____

_____

_____

_____

_____

_____

What keeps you from having more of your ideal weekend:

_____

_____

_____

_____

What will you do about it?

_____

_____

Day 30: Visualization

We all visualize. Our brain naturally thinks in images – this is how we learn. By engaging the right side of your brain more often, you will energize your thinking. Worry is a negative visualization where you replay scenes over and over trying to work it out in your mind.

Just like you learned to breathe deliberately, you are going to use your mind deliberately and focus your thoughts and your emotions on what you want to have happen. We have audio in the online membership that takes you through scenarios to visualize.

When you are ready ...

Find a comfortable place, seated in a chair with your feet on the floor. Loosen any restrictive clothing. Turn off all your devices. Give yourself 15 minutes.

Breathe more slowly and deeply than normal. As you do allow all the tension to drain from your body and let the chair support you completely.

Imagine a movie screen in your mind. See yourself achieving your goal, easily and effortlessly. You have already achieved this goal and you are now watching yourself as you go through each day effortlessly. Enjoy it. Easy. You are so capable. So strong.

Continue to breathe and enjoy this image. Will you allow your mind to continue to work in the background, for as long as it takes for you to achieve your goal?

Wiggle in your chair, come back to the present. Fully and completely awake.

Write out what that experience was like:

_____

_____

_____

_____

_____

Monthly Review:

What worked?

What did not?

What's next?

Tips for the Monthly Review

Congratulations! It has been 30 days since you started this review process. Take the time to review your notes and look for any trends or patterns.

Things that Worked	What Did Not Work	Patterns	Plan
		1.	
		2.	
		3.	
		4.	

Consider the patterns and trends as you think about your next 30 days. What will you do differently?

Day 31: Visualize Your Ideal Day

Begin your morning 15 minutes earlier. Drink 8 ounces of cool water. Engage in the Heart Lock-in for 3minutes. First sending yourself love and appreciation. Then send it out to your workplace and specifically your team. Focus on what you have to do for the day and those people you have important interactions. As you breathe and send them gratitude, see everything working well.

Finish with a reminder to yourself, "Today is a good day."

Drink 4 ounces of water. Head into your day more resilient.

Daily Review:

What worked?

What did not?

What's next?

Day 32: Manage Your Thoughts

Use the practice you did yesterday and start your morning directing your thoughts. As you think about what you have to do today, see it all working out and send the experience love and gratitude.

This is your mission for today - manage your thoughts and focus on what is working well and what you want to have happen.

As your mind drifts and you focus on the negative, use "Getting to Neutral" breathing and unhook from it. Transition into heart focused breathing and release the tension. This reboots your mind and clears the clutter from your thinking.

Practice. Remember, what you focus on grows.

Daily Review:

What worked?

What did not?

What's next?

Day 33: Practice

Use the practice you did yesterday and start your morning directing your thoughts. As you think about what you have to do today, see it all working out and send the experience your love and gratitude.

This is your mission for today - manage your thoughts and focus on what is working well and what you want to have happen.

As your mind drifts and you focus on the negative, use "Getting to Neutral" breathing and unhook from it. Transition into heart focused breathing and release the tension. This reboots your mind and clears the clutter from your thinking.

Practice. Remember, what you focus on grows.

Daily Review:

What worked?

What did not?

What's next?

Day 34: Practice

Use the practice you did yesterday and start your morning directing your thoughts. As you think about what you have to do today, see it all working out and send the experience your love and gratitude.

This is your mission for today - manage your thoughts and focus on what is working well and what you want to have happen.

As your mind drifts and you focus on the negative, use "Getting to Neutral" breathing and unhook from it. Transition into heart focused breathing and release the tension. This reboots your mind and clears the clutter from your thinking.

Practice. Remember, what you focus on grows.

Weekly Review:

What worked?

What did not?

What's next?

Day 35 & 36: A Romantic Weekend

By now you know that weekends need to refresh you and the pace should be slower than your weekday.

Plan a romantic weekend. If you are single you can still do this. Romance is more than chocolates and roses. When people fall in love, they cannot wait to spend time together, they think about what is possible for their future. There is a sense of well-being.

Single or partnered, spend time with the one you love and think about your future. What does it look like? [If single focus on self-acceptance and self-compassion. Do you need to forgive yourself? How do you want to go into your future?]

Write out plans for your romantic weekend:

Day 37: Breathe Deliberately

You are in the final days of your 45-day challenge. We are cycling back and reviewing what we have done so far. Practice your favorite breathing technique that helps you reset and reboot your mind. It could be "Getting to Neutral," Heart Focused Breathing, or Heart Lock-in.

Practice this throughout your day.

Daily Review:

What worked?

What did not?

What's next?

Day 38: Check Your Water Intake

Have you been drinking enough water? If not, here are suggestions to add in additional water:

1. First think in the morning, before any coffee.

2. Before each meal.

3. 2 ounces before meetings.

4. In the afternoon, before you reach for the snickers bar.

5. Before you go to bed.

Daily Review:

What worked?

What did not?

What's next?

Day 39: Practice Gratitude

Review your Gratitude List and think about those things as you practice the Heart Lock-in. Keep this simple and consistent. Doing this activity for 1 minute is powerful and will reset your mood and build up your resilience. This is proven by decades of research.

Practice throughout the day.

Daily Review:

What worked?

What did not?

What's next?

Day 40: Be Mindful (Manage Interruptions)

Mindfulness takes practice and a commitment. The present moment is 3 seconds, you can breathe and focus in 3 seconds and slow down your actions and thoughts. I call this an attention reboot.

What do you notice when you stay in the moment.

This simple process has been found to be restorative and increases your ability to concentrate.

Spend 20 minutes, uninterrupted, reading something, today.

Daily Review:

What worked?

What did not?

What's next?

Day 41: Focus Your Thoughts (Visualize)

Practice visualization. See the day going exactly as you planned. Imagine you handling whatever comes your way. Enjoy that experience, Practice heart focused breathing as you imagine this.

Do this for at least 5 minutes before you start your day.

Weekly Review:

What worked?

What did not?

What's next?

Day 43 & 44: A Reflection Weekend

It is ok to take a weekend off and spend it in quiet reflection or at a slow pace. In fact, it is necessary to have TIME where you can simply be – not compelled to do anything.

Spend time and think about the previous 45 days. What elephants have you eaten and how do you feel about you?

Jot down any thoughts you have.

Day 45: What's Next?

Yay! Congratulations! You have completed this 45-day challenge! It is time for a reward. How will you celebrate?

_____

_____

_____

_____

_____

_____

_____

_____

_____

_____

The next 2 pages give you an opportunity to review the past 45 days and to pull out what you learned and what you want to do more of, as well as those things you will do less.

45-day Review:

What worked?

_____

_____

_____

_____

What did not?

_____

_____

_____

_____

What's next?

_____

_____

_____

_____

Write about your experience. What made the biggest different to you and helped you achieve your goal?

_____

_____

_____

_____

_____

_____

_____

_____

_____

What got in the way of achieving your goal?

_____

_____

_____

_____

_____

_____

_____

Resilience Toolkit

This section includes the instructions for the techniques we discussed in the group. You also have video of these in the online membership.

1. Getting to Neutral

2. Heart Focused Breathing

3. Quick Coherence

4. Heart Lock-in

5. Freeze Frame

HeartMath is a registered trademark of the Institute of HeartMath. emWave, and Personal Stress Reliever are registered trademarks of Quantum Intech, Inc. Quick Coherence is a registered trademark of Doc Childre. Freeze Frame is a registered trademark of the HeartMath Institute

Getting to Neutral

Take a few slow, deep breaths.

In on 4 and out on 4.

Focus on the area around your heart.

As you breathe, focus on the area around your heart.

Continue to breathe in this way.

Continue, concentrating on the area around your heart letting the stressful feeling go, allowing any other thoughts to drift out of your mind.

Heart Focused Breathing

1. Focus your attention in the center of your chest, around your heart.

2. Imagine your breath is flowing is flowing in and through your heart or chest area.

3. Breathe slower and deeper than normal.

Focus your attention on the area of your heart. Imagine your breath is flowing in and out of your chest area; breathing a little slower and deeper than usual.

Suggestion: Inhale 5 seconds, exhale 5 seconds, (or whatever rhythm is comfortable.)

This is the first step in your coherence building tools. It helps you unhook from the stress reaction and the distracting emotions that may have been triggered. This ability to pause, gives you greater flexibility in how you will respond.

Why do we focus our attention on the area of the heart? Research shows that where we focus our attention, physical changes occur in that area. By shifting attention to the heart area, you will shift your heart rhythms into a more coherent state.

Practice using this tool throughout the day. All of these tools have a cumulative effect; the more you use them, the greater impact they will have. And the longer they will have that impact. We have video on the membership site that talks about the research and the impact of these tools. Be sure to visit the site and watch these videos. It will help you understand what a significant difference these tools can make in your life.

Think of something you do frequently during the day. Are you walking down hallways, going to the printer, to a certain department? Practice this technique during that time. Start to associate that activity with Heart Focused Breathing®. It will help you build a new habit!

Quick Coherence

Step 1: Engage Heart Focused Breathing®. Focus your attention on the area of your heart. Imagine your breath is flowing in and out of your chest area, breathing a little slower and deeper than usual.

Suggestion: Inhale 5 seconds, exhale 5 seconds, (or whatever rhythm is comfortable.)

Step 2: Make a sincere attempt to bring up regenerative feelings like appreciation, gratitude, love.

Suggestion: Try to re---experience the feeling you have for someone you love, a pet, a special, an accomplishment, etc., or focus on a feeling of calm or ease.

Coherence is an optimal state when mind, emotions and body are in sync. During the stress reaction, the body is using up fuel to handle the depleting emotions and the physical strain on the body. Renewing emotions create coherence. It is coherence that restores the body and renews the spirit. Be sure to watch the video on the membership site to better understand what is happening in the body and why coherence is so significant.

When would you use this tool? Be sure to practice this when you do not need it! Then use this anytime you want to unhook from a draining emotion, to reset your baseline unhook from a difficult conversation. As with all the tools, use them with your eyes open and you will find you can use them more often. And no one has to know what you are doing!

Heart Lock-in

Step 1: Focus your attention in the area of the heart. Imagine your breath is flowing in and out of your heart or chest area, breathing a little slower and deeper than usual.

Step 2: Activate and sustain a regenerative feeling such as appreciation, care or compassion.

Step 3: Radiate that renewing feeling to yourself and others.

Sustain that feeling for as long as you can working in 1 minute increments.

The Heart Lock In® can be used at the start of your day, business meeting, before tough conversations, any time you want to feel in sync, clear and focused.

Use this when:

- You are struggling with someone and are not sure how to resolve the dilemma.
- You are worried about your family, child, partner.
- You want to reduce wear and tear from unchecked stress from the chaos of the day.
- Any time you want to build a coherent field with teams, families and communities.

Freeze Frame®

This simple process helps you reframe your "stressed" thinking into wiser and more creative solutions. Engage the intelligence of your heart and improve your problem solving, decision making and communication.

Practice "Freeze Frame" and shift your perspective. The worksheet is on the next page.

Step 1

Acknowledge the problem or issue and any attitudes or feelings about it.

Step 2

Focus on the area around your heart. Feel your breath coming into and around your heart. Continue to breathe keeping your focus on the area around your heart.

Step 3

Now, remember a positive feeling or gratitude, appreciation, a genuine feeling about a place, person, or situation. Experience that feeling as fully and deeply as you can.

Step 4

Now going back to your situation (or problem), ask yourself what a more efficient and better attitude would be, what action or feeling would balance and de-stress your system?

Step 5

Notice any shift or change. Your heart's intelligence can come through in subtle and quiet ways.

Freeze Frame Worksheet

Stressful situation:

_____

_____

_____

Current thoughts (head reaction):

_____

_____

_____

After going through Freeze Frame®, what is your intuitive response or "heart's wisdom"?

_____

_____

_____

In doing Freeze Frame, I shifted from _____

_____to _____

About the Author

Cynthia Howard RN, CNC, PhD

Pioneer of the resilient mindset, Dr. Howard has worked with scores of professionals, leaders, and executives to master their mindset and their attention for consistent success.

Cynthia is a Performance Expert and designed a system to produce consistent results.

Dr. Cynthia integrates the latest research in the fields of flow, resilience, emotional intelligence, and high performance within the structure of Lean and Six sigma. This combination offers rapid, lasting change.

To contact Cynthia about this program, speaking at your organization, or for a consultation to use lean principles, email drh@eileadership.org.

www.eileadership.org

Work Smart Club

Our online Center for Work and Well-Being offers training in leadership, productivity, stress management, emotional intelligence, leading through change, problem solving and lean sigma tools.

Our courses are short, easy to consume on the go, covering topics to help you get more done, balance work and life, strengthen your leadership, eliminate stress and support your well-being.

We offer a library of premium resources with video, audio, templates, checklists, guidebooks and live and online support.

Visit www.worksmart.club.

www.worksmart.club | worksmart thinkdifferent

Ei Leadership

Ei Leadership provides innovative executive and organizational development, consulting, and leadership training, utilizing Emotional Intelligence (Ei) tools and practices. We assess, coach, and train for resilient thinking using Ei, resilience strategies, and the Lean Six Sigma process.

Contact us today and schedule a complimentary session to find out what program is best for you and your work group.

www.eileadership.org

Here is what one participant has said:

> *"This program changed my life. I have concrete tools I can use with my team and I have finally learned to honor my strengths. This confidence takes the struggle out of my day since I no longer have to second guess myself."*

—Danielle F., DNP, Director of Emergency Services

Coaching is the single greatest accelerator for change.